Good Mortgage Advice:
The Home Buyer's Guide to
Financing a Home –
A Crash Course for Confidence

This book is dedicated to all those who

believe in the dream of home ownership!

- *M.D. Baltazar*

Specially dedicated to:

_____

From your trusted friend:

_____

GOOD MORTGAGE ADVICE:

THE HOME BUYER'S GUIDE TO FINANCING A HOME - A CRASH COURSE FOR CONFIDENCE

First edition. March 31, 2016.

Written by M. D. Baltazar

Table of Contents

Chapter 1: Let's introduce you to the key members of the financing process

1. *Mortgage Company:* A mortgage loan is a loan that is secured by real or personal property. In this book, we will often call these home loans. The mortgage company that grants these loans is often referred to as the lender. It is quite common that the lender that processes your loan will sell it to another mortgage company for servicing.

2. *Loan Officer:* This person takes your personal information for the loan application (in person, by phone or online), pulls your credit and gets a decision on your application. If you are prequalified, then your loan officer will let you know what documentation is needed to verify the information you provided on the application. This person can also be referred to as a lender.

3. *Processor:* This person helps the loan officer put your loan file together for underwriting. The better the processor, the more you will interact with this person. Otherwise, you may find that your loan officer is doing a lot of the administrative parts of the loan process. This is not necessarily a bad thing, but something to keep an eye on because you want you want your loan officer to be focused on the more specialized tasks. Plus, it is also important to have your loan officer or processor available so you can ask questions along the way.

4. *Underwriter:* This person has the final say on loan applications. An underwriter reviews the documentation provided in the loan file and makes sure that it meets the loan requirements. Oftentimes, the underwriter will request more supporting documentation than what the loan officer/processor thought was needed to meet loan requirements. This is totally alright, even if it can be a bit of a nuisance. (*Note: if an underwriter approves a loan that does not meet loan requirements and it is caught after the new loan goes into effect, this could cause the lender to incur significant costs/penalties and even a bad reputation.*)

5. *Appraiser:* Certified or licensed person who provides a professional opinion of the value of the subject property. This person is usually paid upfront by the loan applicant, through the selected lender. An appraisal report is required to finance a home; it is a great tool used to make sure that you are not overpaying for a home while ensuring your lender that the home's value is sufficient.

6. *Attorney/Title Company:* Depending on the state you are buying in, this 3rd party company assists with the transfer of ownership for the subject property. They will research the property for liens and help ensure a proper transfer. In the case where a title insurance company is used, they actually issue an insurance policy that protects the lender/buyer from any liens missed that "cloud" the title.

7. *Home Insurance Company:* Like auto insurance, you are required to maintain hazard insurance on the collateral being used to secure the loan. As long as you are not buying a property within a Homeowners Association that provides a blanket insurance policy on all of its units, you get to select the insurance company.

Now that you have met some of the people you will encounter along the way, let's look into some key factors of the home loan application.

Chapter 2: The three-legged stool: credit, income and down payment

Why such an analogy? A three-legged stool cannot stand up with one of its legs missing, and so is the case with the home loan application process. It cannot be approved if one of these three "legs" has an issue: credit, income or down payment. Now let's take a look at each of these in more detail.

First Leg: Establishing, understanding
& enhancing your credit

When I was a kid, my grandfather told me that borrowing money was bad. He said that if I couldn't pay cash for it, then I didn't need it. While this was loving advice, it does not help someone trying to qualify for a home loan today. You see, you need this thing called "credit" in order to qualify for the best financing options available. For example, while there are FHA loans available for people without credit, there is a required mortgage insurance premium (MIP) that is added to the monthly payment for this type of loan. For an applicant with a good credit score, a conventional loan would have an MIP with better terms. We will discuss FHA and conventional loans in more depth later on. We will also learn more about mortgage insurance and loan payments. For now, let's continue to talk about credit. We are just getting started!

More information on establishing credit can be found in Appendix A.

Credit scores are used to determine risk and are provided by the three major credit reporting agencies: Transunion, Equifax and Experian. Each of these agencies has its own credit scoring formula and provides a different score. Besides the different formulas, the credit scores can also differ due to some credit accounts not reporting to all three agencies. When applying for a home loan, the lender will obtain all three scores, drop the high and low scores, and use the middle score to qualify the application. As you can imagine, this initial component of the application process is critical and can determine upfront which loan options are not going to be available.

It is important to note that credit repair services are being marketed more and more these days, but the advice can be inconsistent, ineffective and costly. Be very careful when you are buying credit repair services. Also, getting your credit score on your own can be misleading. Therefore, it is highly recommended that you get your credit score directly from a mortgage lender.

The following breakdown shows what is factored into credit scoring and how each is weighted:

Payment History: 35%, Amount Owed: 30%, Length of Credit History: 15%, New Credit: 10%, Types of Credit: 10%

Let's take a closer look at these major factors that contribute to your credit score, starting with Payment History. There is no better way to determine credit risk than to see how someone is paying their debts. If your neighbor wanted to borrow $20, but still had not returned the $10 from last month, then chances are that you do not want to lend him anything else. Wouldn't it have been nice to know in advance that your neighbor had a bad history of paying people back? Well, credit reports are a historical record of how you have paid your creditors and help tell future creditors about you.

Being late on some payments, for example, throws up a red flag that you may have budgeting issues. Of course, there can be valid reasons behind the late payments, like illness, death in the family or a job loss that was outside of your control. Lenders can take things like this into account when processing an application for someone with less than perfect credit. While having valid reasons behind the bad credit will not change your credit scores, it could still possibly open up some loan options. Later in this book, we will look at various loan options that may be available to people with bad credit, poor credit and all the way up to excellent credit.

Amount Owed, another great way to help determine risk, is also reflected in a person's credit score. Think about it this way: If somebody has all six of their credit cards maxed out, do you think they are really ready to take on the added responsibility of a house payment? In this scenario, the maxed credit cards communicate to the credit reporting agencies that the consumer has budgeting issues and may have become dependent on credit cards as a source of sustainability. Since this consumer is likely to become delinquent once the "source" is no longer available, the credit risk is higher and lowers the credit scores for this person, which translates into being a credit risk. Unfortunately, this scenario is quite common and often leads to bankruptcy.

Therefore, the Amount Owed category is given a lot of weight. This category also takes into account the number of revolving accounts with balances and how much of each account is being used. It is important to keep your credit card balances to less than 50% of the credit limit. For example, if you have a $1,000 credit limit, you should keep your balance under $500 (50%). Once you go above the 50% mark, your credit scores will begin to drop. Here is another interesting fact: Most people think that their credit score gets better when they pay off a credit card, but this is not the case. When you have a balance more than $0 but less than 30%, you get "bonus points" on your credit scores. The *bonus* is even bigger when the balance is less than 10%, which is why we advise in Appendix A to keep a balance of less than $30 on a $300 secured credit card.

Now we are moving on to the three smaller categories in our chart, which together make up less of an impact on credit than each of the two we just discussed. These categories are still very important, however, and can separate scores that are in the 600's from those that are in the 700's. To illustrate these categories, let's imagine that the creditors are thinking of "marrying" the borrowers but want to know more about their character first. For example, the Length of Credit History is important because it exhibits stability. If someone has three accounts reflected on their credit report, with the oldest account being 18 months old, then this is a person who has limited experience with debt. This limited experience is due to not having very much data available, which makes it a lot harder to get a better risk assessment than if the person had 10 years of credit history. Like anyone else, creditors would rather "marry" someone they know more about, instead of a virtual stranger.

The same goes for New Credit. While it is a very good sign that someone trusts that person enough to approve them for credit, it may still be too early to judge how they will manage that account. Also keep in mind that every time you apply for credit, your credit is checked, which is reported as an inquiry on your credit. Minimizing your credit inquiries is very important because inquiries do drop your credit scores; the more inquiries in a short period of time (i.e., 30 days), the bigger the impact of each subsequent inquiry. The way creditors view excessive inquiries is that the consumer is desperate and/or does not know enough about credit to respect it. Revisiting the "marriage" metaphor, let's imagine it this way: It is not a good feeling when a creditor receives a proposal from a potential borrower who has proposed to five other creditors in the last month. Chances are that the borrower is being declined for a reason and/or that they are taking on too many obligations at once. This is a potential warning sign, so the credit reporting agencies will reduce the borrower's credit scores to alert creditors that the borrower may have become riskier. Therefore, not having your credit pulled too much is a good rule to follow.

Finally, the Types of Credit being used also have an impact on credit scores. The best type of credit is a secured installment loan. There are two reasons that this type of account is best. First, it is secured by an asset. This not only minimizes the risk for the creditor, but it also signals to future creditors that the borrower has assets to pledge in the first place. Second, an installment loan's balance is designed to go down and be eliminated within a certain period of time. Examples of this type of account are home and auto loans. The next best type of credit is an unsecured installment loan, which is due to the fact that the balance is scheduled to be paid off. The final credit type is a revolving credit, which can be a credit card or department store card. This type of credit is deemed riskier because it is not designed to be eliminated; you can use it whenever you want to. There is an added risk by the fact that revolving credit is often used when there is a lack of income and/or savings, which would further strain consumers' ability to afford their debts. When someone begins "robbing Peter to pay Paul," this begins a vicious cycle that can be hard to get out of and often leads to bankruptcy.

As you can imagine, there are more things that can hurt one's credit than there are to help it, but taking a proactive approach to managing and utilizing credit can really work in your favor.

Appendix C has more tips on maintaining and improving scores.

Second Leg: Critical income factors to keep in mind

Just like credit, when it comes to a home loan application, there are more things that can hurt one's income situation than can help it. Before we go into a few examples, let's start by looking at what lenders would like to see. Lenders like to see at least two years with the present employer and steady income that is trending upwards and easy to verify. This seems simple enough, right? Well, unfortunately, it can get complicated very quickly.

Here are a few of the hundreds of possible complications that can arise:

1. Job changes with a NEW line of work (changes within same line of work are just fine)
2. Full-time but working less than "full time" hours (looks like a part-time worker)
3. Unpaid time off (this may be worked around with proper documentation)
4. Commission-based for less than two years (need to show a commission history of at least two years)
5. Laid off and/or seasonal worker (this may work with history of at least two years)
6. Signs of an income drop over the last two years (this would be seen on tax returns)

7. Inconsistent bonus or overtime income over the last two years (may be possible to average this)

8. Unreimbursed job-related expenses on tax returns (while this does reduce your taxable income, it may also reduce the amount of income you can report on a loan application)

9. Recently retired with no regularly scheduled income (and/or the income will stop in less than three years – proving three years of continuing income is required for most financing)

10. Receiving child support that is not court-ordered (and/or the child support will stop in less than three years)

   Note: Please do not confuse the three-year requirement for fixed income with the two year used for wage earners.

Not everyone is going to have a perfect income history. Most lenders are usually prepared to work with unique scenarios requiring more attention. This is accomplished by putting together conclusive documentation to make a case for a loan's approval. Documentation is critical to just about every aspect of the loan approval process, but is even bigger when it comes to income verification. While there can be many ways to conclusively document most scenarios, there are some, such as being commission-based for less than two years, that are presently "set in stone" as a loan requirement. In theory, lending authorities want to see a two-year track record displayed in order to use an income stream. Two other examples along these same lines are bonus and overtime income. It is safe to say that using a base income (salary or a guaranteed 40-hour workweek schedule) for income qualification works best, but of course, being able to report more income does increase the loan approval amount.

Borrowers with unique scenarios would be wise to request that their loan officer get the opinion of the loan underwriter upfront, in order to validate the income being used for the application before getting too far into the home buying process. Unfortunately, some loan officers guess and overestimate the income figures that the underwriter is able to use. When this happens midway through the process, the borrower loses the home they are trying to buy and the money invested upfront. By simply knowing that you can request an upfront income review by an underwriter, you are now a much savvier consumer.

Since there are literally hundreds of possible scenarios that can arise, try to make sure your lender is on top of things. We will discuss ways to search for a lender later in this book. Please keep in mind that there are resources available at GoodMortgageAdvice.com that can help as well.

Third Leg: Understanding down payment options & requirements

While obtainable, it does take hard work and dedication to establish and maintain good credit and income. But let's not forget that we are building a three-legged stool and there is another "leg" to consider: Down payment. It is important to note that while a down payment is required for most loan programs; other funds are needed when buying a home. There are still closing costs, escrows and prepaids to be paid at closing. Even a 0% down loan requires additional funds. So, having those funds available can be critical. In this section, we are going to provide a few examples of popular loan programs and their minimum down payment requirements.

No Money Down Loans

The two most popular no money down programs are VA and USDA. The VA (Veterans Administration) loan is only available to members of the military, veterans of military service, and sometimes to the widows of late veterans. Loan qualifications still need to be met by the VA-eligible applicant. While this type of loan does not have a down payment requirement, the applicant still has the opportunity to put money down if desired. This not only reduces the amount being financed, but could also reduce the amount of the associated VA fees. Another huge benefit of this type of loan is that there is no monthly mortgage insurance (MI) premium included in the monthly payment.

The USDA (United States Department of Agriculture) loan is reserved for qualified applicants who buy a home within certain areas designated by the USDA. While this program does not have a down payment requirement, it does have a monthly mortgage insurance requirement.

See Appendix E for more information on MI.

Low Money Down Loans

For first-time homebuyers (or anyone who hasn't owned a home for the last three years), there is a 3% down payment option for a conventional loan. While this does help the borrower with limited funds for a down payment, the cost of the monthly mortgage insurance is higher on a 3% down payment than when 5% is put down for this type of financing.

FHA financing is the next lowest, with a 3.5% down payment requirement. One of the drawbacks to the FHA loan is that the monthly mortgage insurance never falls off of the loan, unless a down payment of 10% or more is made. The only way to get rid of this type of MI is to refinance or payoff the FHA loan. The most popular alternative to an FHA loan is a conventional loan.

While one may assume that the 3% conventional loan option is always better than the 3.5% FHA loan, keep in mind that the circumstances for each applicant can be very different. Every applicant may have a different goal. There may even be loan qualifying restrictions that can impact which option an applicant takes. Regardless, this is why you need to have a trustworthy and experienced loan officer to turn to for these important decisions.

What is the best down payment option?

Assuming that the borrower has the money to put down, 20% is the magic number when it comes to having the best down payment. This amount eliminates the mortgage insurance requirement on conventional loans. Keep in mind, when someone puts 20% down on an

FHA loan, there is still going to be monthly mortgage insurance for the first 11 years of the loan. While the elimination of mortgage insurance from the monthly mortgage payment is a nice savings to have, a 20% down payment can often be too large. So there can be many reasons to put less than 20% down and pay for the required mortgage insurance. In the next chapter, we will learn a little bit more about these programs, as well as some other loan options.

Chapter 3: Understanding more about the various loan options available

Buying a home is a huge accomplishment, and if you have read this far, you have proven that you are serious about buying a home and fulfilling the American dream of home ownership. We have provided a lot of background on what goes into home financing. In this chapter, we are going to learn a little bit more about the main loan options mentioned previously. We will also look at a couple of less common loan types that help in different ways. While we cannot cover every aspect of each loan, we can give you a general idea of what each loan entails. The goal of this section is to familiarize you with available loan options to give you confidence on your home buying journey.

Bonus Section: Understanding PITI

When I first started in the mortgage business in 1997, I was surprised by the number of acronyms that were part of the everyday home loan lingo. I had to keep a notebook that translated them all. So please do not be discouraged by all of the acronyms that you will come across. There is a special Acronyms section in the back of this book to help with a few of the more common ones. For now, we are going to talk about PITI because this is what comprises a mortgage payment and is used to compare various loan options.

PITI is an acronym for Principal, Interest, Taxes and Insurances. These are the items that can comprise your monthly mortgage payment. The loan itself has scheduled monthly payments which pay down part of the loan's principal. Each loan payment also includes charges for the interest accrued since the last payment – this is the "P & I." In order to pay for the property taxes and insurances (T/I) for the home when due, the lender will create an escrow account to hold the funds collected from the borrower. Part of these funds is collected upfront when the loan is taken out, and the rest is collected on a monthly basis. Since the tax and insurance figures can change over time, the lender will review the loan's escrow account annually and adjust accordingly. This is called an Annual Escrow Analysis. If you overpaid your escrow account the previous year, then you will get a check in the mail; if your account is underpaid, you will have to cover the shortage. This can be done by paying the shortage upfront, or including it in your mortgage payment and paying it over time. Even if you pay the shortage upfront, the new payment will still be higher than the year before to account for the higher taxes and/or insurances on your home.

For conventional loans with 20% down, the borrower is given the option to pay the property taxes and home insurances on their own and not include them in their mortgage payment. While some borrowers prefer to pay on their own, most still opt to have them both as a part of their monthly payment for convenience and/or budgeting purposes. Either way, it is good to keep this option in mind. This information is helpful to have bookmarked for later, after you have purchased a home.

Now let's take a look at the different loan options available.

FHA/VA/USDA loan

We touched on some of the main points for each of these loan options while learning about the third leg of the stool, which covered down payment options. Let's address a few more key points for these government loans. First, FHA loans are the most popular because they can be used by any borrower and are not limited to a certain group (like the VA loan).

Second, all three government loans also have more lenient qualification requirements than those for conventional loans, although FHA and VA loans do have lower loan limits. The USDA loan does not have loan limits but does have income limits, which ultimately limits the loan amount. Also, this loan is restricted to certain areas, which can be found at USDA.gov.

Third, all three government loans are limited to buying a primary residence only. A different loan option would be needed to buy a vacation or investment home.

Finally, in Appendix D, where we review the wait times required when buying a home after a bankruptcy, short-sale or foreclosure, you will notice that these three loans have shorter wait times than conventional loans.

Conventional loan

Just because conventional financing is not "as lenient" as the government loans does not make it a less desirable loan option. In many ways, the conventional loan can be the best loan option available. For example, the government loans just mentioned all have large upfront fees associated with them; these fees are not charged on conventional loans (or the next two loans we will be discussing). Another example is the fact that a conventional loan's mortgage insurance premium eventually falls off of the PITI payment, while it may never fall off of an FHA or USDA loan. Due to these factors, conventional financing is often the most cost effective loan option available.

It is important to note that up to this point, we have discussed the most commonly used loans on the market, all of which are backed by the government and/or Wall Street investors. It is also important to note that while the payments for all of these loans are being made to mortgage companies, it is not those mortgage companies' money being lent to the borrowers. The funds are really supplied by investors; the mortgage companies are paid to service these loans and collect payments. This information will help to better understand the next two loan options we will be learning about.

Portfolio loan

Before the government created Fannie Mae and Freddie Mac for conventional financing, it was up to local banks to help finance the American dream of homeownership. When banks and mortgage companies lend out their own money and do not share the risk with the government or investors, this introduces another type of loan – the portfolio loan. These types of loans do not have to comply with the stringent requirements set forth by the aforementioned loan options, but typically do come with higher minimum down payment requirements. The main reason for this is because there is no mortgage insurance to help offset the risk taken by the lending institution.

These requirements are independently determined by the lending institutions themselves. Another important factor to consider for portfolio loans is that they typically have higher interest rates. Portfolio lending is still done throughout America, but it is even more prevalent in certain communities and areas with special characteristics. This type of loan is a great option to have when you can afford to finance a home, but do not meet the stringent requirements for the more commonly used loan options.

Private money loan

This last loan type is quickly becoming more popular in many parts of the country, but it has been around since the beginning of time. This is the classic loan from someone in the community – the private money loan. These loans are from private investors who help create homeownership when everyone else says no. Like portfolio lending, these loans have higher down payment requirements than conventional and government loans.

Another aspect of these loans is that the interest rates tend to be even higher than those on portfolio loans. This is due to the fact that most private money lenders do not carry as many loans as the larger institutions, which makes them less diversified and subject to more risk on an individual basis. Regardless, they help fulfill a need in the home financing industry. Private lending is not usually intended for the long term and can have a demand feature after one to three years, which would require the loan to be refinanced or paid off by selling the home.

Middle of the Book Checkpoint

Up to this point, we have touched on many key factors that go into the loan process. Understanding these mechanics is a great first step towards putting a solid game plan in place and preparing for a home purchase. Now let's switch gears and move towards the psychological factors involved in the home loan process.

Chapter 4: Three costly misconceptions about financing a home

First Misconception: All lenders are the same

As much as I wish this were true, this could not be the further from the truth. First off, let's point out that there are two distinct lenders being referenced here, the loan officer and there is the company that the loan officer works for. Both carry the label of "lender" and both can vary dramatically from others. Let me put it to you this way: there are some great people (some may even be close friends and family) who are not very good lenders, while there are some not so good people who make very good lenders. Let's put some of these combinations into groups and analyze each:

- *The good person but bad lender:* This is a loan officer who means well, but is not fully equipped to be successful. They may be educated, but lack knowledge about lending rules, guidelines and processes. Perhaps they lack the support necessary to get the job done effectively. Their shortcomings may cause delays, or even cause you to lose the opportunity to buy. Exercise caution when trusting this person professionally.

- *The bad person but "good" lender:* This is the loan officer who knows how to get the job done. So where is the harm in working with this person? Isn't getting approved the goal? Well, bad people do bad things. If this loan officer is a bad person, maybe he is cheating his way into getting the loan done. While most home buyers just want to get approved, participating in a loan that is falsely represented and approved with misinformation is loan fraud and a federal offense. Trust your instincts and stay away from the loan officer that "can get it all done" regardless of ethics.

- *The good person who is a good lender:* This is the loan officer who is like a best friend. They can be very open with you, very direct with you and always look out for your best interests. Sometimes when we are told no, we get upset. But at the end of the day, we should understand that "no" may have been the best thing that could have ever happened to us. A good lender wouldn't necessarily say "no" to someone's loan application. A good lender would say "not now" and then proceed to put together a game plan and advise how the loan could be approved in a clean and legal way.

Let's look at a few helpful hints that can help you find the right loan officer:

1. *The loan officer has a support stuff -- period.* If your loan officer has an assistant, their own processor, their own underwriter and they all work together under the same roof, then your loan officer has an army working for you. This greatly enhances your success factor!

2. *The loan officer has a great support staff.* You can only be as strong as your weakest link, and if you have a member of your loan officer's team who drops the ball, it could cost you your loan.

3. *Be careful of the loan officer who claims to have all this help, but still has to call out-of-town to talk to their processor or call out-of-state to talk to their underwriter.* If they are misrepresenting their team to you, then what else are they misrepresenting?

4. *Experience matters!* Make sure that your loan officer has the experience necessary to get the job done. Feel free to interview them and ask them what separates them from the competition. If most of their answers do not center on their experience level, then proceed with caution. I'm sorry, but being a parent of three does not necessarily help get the loan done more efficiently!

5. *Most importantly, make sure your loan officer has a mortgage license.* A licensed loan officer not only has to pass a background check for licensing, but must also take several hours of required training and pass rigorous state and federal tests. In addition, several hours of continuing education are required every year for license renewal. This alone helps to make it easier for you to not worry too much about #4.

Let's discuss how the company the loan officer works for factors into your decision. As you can imagine, not all companies are the same. Some have a great reputation for good service, while others have a great reputation for community involvement. Some companies can brag about having the most home loans in the country, while others get special awards and recognition. At the end of the day, none of this helps you get your loan approved. Your loan officer can only be as good as the company he or she works for. Here are a few tips on how to find a company that is perfect for you:

- *Statistics:* Let the numbers speak for themselves. Lending statistics are a great way to see which companies are doing the most loans in your community. This makes it very easy to see who is really getting the job done in your area. Beware: A company claiming to have the most loans in your area does NOT mean that they processed those loans to begin with. They may have just bought them from another lender.
- *Friends:* If working with a local lender is important, then asking your friends, family and co-workers is a good start to finding a possible lender. You still need to double-check and make sure they meet your expectations and requirements, though.
- *The pros:* Another great way to find out who is highly recommended in your area is to ask your real estate professional, accountant or title company. The chances are very good that these professionals have come into contact with

numerous lenders over time, know who works well and can be an excellent resource. Still apply what you know and double-check the loan officer anyway. It is better to be safe than sorry!

Second Misconception: I shouldn't apply for a loan until I have saved up enough money

The truth of the matter is that you should apply as soon as you decide that you want to own a home. Even if you are at the beginning of a 12-month lease, you should still apply. Even if you have bad credit or income issues, you should still apply sooner rather than later. By applying early, you can find out exactly where you stand today. As long as you are working with a good lender, then you should get a solid game plan to help you accomplish your homeownership goals.

Let's look at a few possible scenarios:

1. *You get approved today and knew you would... so now what?* Congratulations! You have a lot to be proud of. Now you can plan for the next phase and take into account the following factors: How much are you qualified for? How much do you need to put down? What the payments would be based on the present market rates, and what you can buy? Having this information helps you to put things into better perspective as you begin to look at the inventory, mortgage rate trends and other relevant information.

2. *You did not get approved but you thought you would...* there is no need to panic. Again, this is why you should apply early. At

this point, you will need to find out what needs to be addressed. Hopefully, it's a simple credit or income issue that can be fixed before buying. By applying early, you put time on your side and avoid having to delay your homeownership dreams and goals.

3. *You didn't think you would be approved right away, but you are!* I love it when this happens. A person drums up enough courage to apply and fears those dreaded words "I'm sorry," but ends up being surprised to hear the word "congratulations!" This actually happens a lot and truly illuminates the American spirit that is embedded in homeownership. Although this scenario is fun to talk about, you have to stop and wonder: How many other people want to buy a home and would qualify if they applied, but never apply because they fear being rejected? That is a very sad fact to think about! Check out my eBook *Overcoming the Mindset of a Chronic Renter*, for more background on this scenario.

4. *You knew you would not be approved and you were not... but have a plan now!* You are now better off than when you started. You have a game plan to work on. I would venture a guess that this scenario represents almost half of all home loan applications. This is perfectly okay. What is *not* okay is when applicants do not follow through on their game plans. Those who stick to their plan and become homeowners as a result get to feel that great sense of achievement like no other!

5. *You applied, received the results but do not think your loan officer got it right.* Listen. I get it. You are not a loan officer and do not feel qualified to second-guess the loan officer who you trusted and chose to apply with. But if you do not have a good feeling about your lender, the results, or how the process was handled, then you absolutely must get a second opinion. Like many things in life, it is important to trust your gut and act on it. You would be surprised how many times I have personally helped people who were not handled properly. Either they were declined when they should have been approved, were approved for less than they should have been, or were asked to unknowingly commit fraud! Be wise. Be careful.

Third Misconception: If I am unaware that it is fraud, it is not fraud

If it seems like I am beating a dead horse here, so be it. Honestly, I really cannot stress enough how serious a crime mortgage fraud is. Fraud can come in many different forms – it can be blatant, or seem too small to matter. But fraud is fraud. The definition is quite simple: *deception intended to result in financial or personal gain.*

To protect yourself, it is important to keep this rule in mind: If it is not true, do not say it or sign it.

Loan requirements were put in place to help determine who can qualify and for how much. It helps ensure that the borrower can effectively afford a home. Many people are willing to do whatever it takes to get approved, which can be dangerous. As you pursue your dreams of homeownership, please keep in mind that it will all happen exactly how it is supposed to happen. If you do not meet the approval requirements, then learn more about the reasons for that and redraw your game plan.

Being declined doesn't mean you cannot ever get your dream home; it just means that you have some work to do before it is time. But I promise that you do not want to learn the hard way by lying for your loan approval – prison is not worth it. So, if you have a lender who is asking you to lie, fib or stretch the truth, then fire them immediately! You can work with a more caring and truthful loan officer. You can thank yourself later!

Chapter 5: Ten critical mistakes to avoid while choosing a lender

As we begin to wind down this book and set you off on your journey towards the American dream of homeownership, let's quickly outline some critical mistakes that can hinder your journey:

1. *Taking a recommendation from an unqualified source:* While advice is great to receive from loved ones and people close to you, please keep in mind that you now have an understanding of what goes into the home loan process. This increased knowledge and understanding will help you find the right lender and hold this lender accountable. Once you have selected your lender, you need to trust your lender. And unless grandma is a qualified lender, it is good to take what she says with a grain of salt and trust the lender you have hired.

2. *Allowing every lender that you meet to pull your credit:* Every lender that you talk to is going to want to pull your credit. That is because it gives them a sense of commitment from you. But during your initial search for a lender, as you try to identify the right one for you, you only need their quotes, advice, opinions and/or assessment of your application information. Therefore, you should only allow one lender to pull your credit during your initial search for a lender. Before you apply with this first lender, make sure they are willing to give you a copy of your tri-

merge credit report so that you can share the information with the other lenders that you talk to. Keep in mind, if you do not stay with the first lender who pulled your credit report initially, you will eventually need to allow the lender you select for your loan to pull a credit report on you.

3. *Using an online credit report or credit score:* Did you know that there are different versions of your credit report? There are versions used for credit card lending, auto loans, and home loans. You want to use the most accurate data while you are shopping around and researching your options. Get the mortgage version of your report. See Point 2 (above), as well as Appendix B, which talks more about this.

4. *Letting lenders convince you that they cannot help you unless they pull your credit:* A lender can use the data from the tri-merge report you provide to them for a thorough analysis. They may not be able to get an automated decision on your loan application, but they can still provide you with the information you are looking for: qualification amount, interest rate and loan options. If you come across a lender who says they have to pull their own report upfront, then this is a great time to fire them and move on to the next.

5. *Thinking that all lenders have the same criteria for loan approvals:* Some lenders have overlays, while others may not. An overlay is an added loan requirement from the lender that is not specifically a conventional or government loan

requirement. Overlays are used by lenders to improve the quality of their borrowers by implementing stricter conditions to qualify. While it is not easy for "the average Joe" to determine who has the overlays and who doesn't, this is where getting a second opinion can be important. Again, if you do not feel good about your application results, then trust that inner voice and act accordingly.

6. *Choosing a lender solely on rate – not on value:* Although, getting the best rate is very important, getting the loan done right is even more important. As I mentioned earlier, you would be surprised how many people I have helped get their loan done correctly. Remember: the rate is meaningless if you do not get the loan done right or done at all!

7. *Choosing a lender because that is where you bank:* Relationships are important, but they should not cloud your judgment. Sometimes you can find a better than your bank. That doesn't mean you have to close your accounts. It just means that you found a more qualified loan officer.

8. *Choosing a lender because it has good advertising:* Remember to let your lender serve you and not sell you. While advertising can be a positive sign and provide valuable information, you should still select a lender for better reasons than something visually or audibly appealing.

9. *Using the same person that your friend used:* These types of recommendations are great to have, but you have to weigh

them with all of the other information you now have. It is quite possible that your friend did not take the proper steps when selecting their lender. Maybe next time, you will be the one referring someone to them. So, be sure to take into account everything you have learned, and avoid cutting corners.

10. *Not researching your loan officer prospects on the NMLS Consumer Access:* NMLS stands for Nationwide Multistate Licensing System. If you select a licensed mortgage loan officer, then you can visit http://www.nmlsconsumeraccess.org/ and see their profile, job history, and licensing history, as well as any disciplinary actions taken against the loan officer.

Chapter 6: The three questions to ask yourself before you apply for a home loan

Pat yourself on the back! You are now one chapter away from starting your journey towards the American dream of homeownership. In the first few chapters of this book, we took a look at some of the mechanics that go into the home loan application. Then we took a look at some of the psychology involved in the process. In this final chapter, we are going to do a quick soul check. This is a simple and very important step because buying a home will be one of the biggest investments you will ever make. You want your mind, body and soul fully committed to this endeavor. Now, let's take out a notebook and write down the answers to these three questions.

1. What are your main reasons for buying a new home?
2. Do you believe in the American dream of homeownership?
3. What do you feel inside when you say "I am going to own a new home"?

Close your eyes and try to imagine that day when you receive the keys to your new home. This home belongs to you. This is a home that you can do anything with (as long as you have the proper permits, when required). It is the place where you will create memories and build a better tomorrow. You feel a sense of accomplishment, and this will fuel your confidence for many years to come. Best of all, you do not have to pay rent to someone else who is already benefiting from the American dream of homeownership!

The American dream question may be a loaded one, but you would be surprised to know the number of "chronic renters" who live in America today. Chronic renters are people who fully qualify for a home but prefer to rent. While there are valid reasons for renting (e.g., job, family, health), many Americans prefer to rent due to fear or a bad past experience. I analyze these reasons and others in my eBook, *Overcoming the Mindset of a Chronic Renter*. Truth is that homeownership is not for everyone, but it is a dream that everyone can pursue.

In the last soul check question, the answers will mean more to you than to anyone else. Only you know your hopes, dreams, and goals. Still, this can be valuable information for others. Feel free to share this with your loan officer, your real estate agent or even friends who need encouragement of their own. Positive dreams, goals and aspirations are contagious and can only make the world a better place. Now, it is time to find your place!

Congratulations! You are now ready to start your journey. While you will always continue to learn more and more about home loans and homeownership over time, you now have a great foundation from which to launch. Good luck and God bless!

APPENDIX A: Establishing credit

A common frustration with credit is that many people are declined for credit due to a lack of credit history. But if you need to have credit to be approved for credit, then where do you begin? Here are the top three ways to get started:

1. Get added as an authorized user on someone else's credit card (usually family).
   a. This will allow you to use the credit history of that card, as it will be placed on your credit history. This can backfire, however, if the person holding that card becomes delinquent in making payments.
   b. It could take a few months for this account to populate on your credit report.
   c. This strategy will increase the probability that you will be approved for an account of your own.
   d. Once you have established your own accounts for at least 12+ months, you should request to be removed as an authorized user (in order to remove the risk of delinquency).
2. Open a secured credit card in your name only (usually a $300 limit). For a secured credit card, you deposit $300 as collateral with the bank granting the credit card. You are basically borrowing your own money while paying interest to the bank.

Even though it may sound a little backwards, this is a very common method used to help establish credit. Here are a few helpful tips:

    a. This type of card should be used to establish credit *only*.

    b. Depending on your bank, you may be able to convert your secured card into an unsecured card after a year. When this happens, your $300 initial deposit will be returned to you.

    c. Should this account become delinquent, the bank can close the account and use your initial deposit to help pay off the balance on the card.

    d. To maximize your credit score with this account, keep your balance less than 10% of the credit available (e.g., less than $30 on a $300 limit). If you do not think this makes sense, please re-read "a."

3. Get a co-signer. A co-signer is a qualified applicant who signs with an unqualified applicant to get the application approved. This is common with both auto and home loans.

    a. If you are hoping to buy a home within the next couple of years, then you may want to reconsider financing a new car. Car payments can be high and will limit your buying power when it is time to buy a home.

    b. A qualified co-signer can be used to buy a home with an FHA loan. This will allow for the purchase of a home sooner rather than later.

c. In most cases, the co-signer will need to qualify for the new loan on their own before they can help someone else qualify. For example, if Mom has an 800 credit score but does not have verifiable income, then she may be declined herself.

APPENDIX B: Getting your credit report and knowing what good credit looks like

As mentioned in Chapter 5, it is important to get a mortgage version of your credit report, and not the ones you can get online. This is important because the credit scores used in the mortgage industry are different than those used in the auto lending and credit card industries. As mentioned earlier, applicants who think all credit scores are the same (even those you can buy online) are usually in for a surprise and a lot of unnecessary confusion.

The best way to get such a copy is to apply with a lender who is willing to share the tri-merge credit report with you. What does "tri-merge" mean? Tri-merge simply means that it has the three major bureaus on the one report. If they say they can't or won't, move on to the next lender. You want to get a copy of the mortgage version of your credit report that you can share with other lenders for quotes and assessments. This tri-merge report will have your debts, credit scores and all the relevant information needed for a good consultation.

So, what does good credit look like? This is a tricky question because it partly depends on the type of loan you are trying to get. It also depends on how the various mortgage lenders want to price their loans. Some lenders may penalize someone with a lower credit score while other lenders may not. For now, let's just note that good credit is a relative term.

So that we give ourselves an idea of what to expect, let's give ourselves some generic benchmarks to work with. First, credit scores below 600 can safely be considered bad credit. And guess what? FHA and VA financing can go down to a credit score of 580! So again, bad credit is a relative term. Most lenders do, however, require a credit score of at least 600 or 620. This requirement is called an *overlay* and is also mentioned in Chapter 5. This is another reason to get your credit report upfront and shop around. Feel free to email me (Contact@BaltazarPartners.com) with any questions you may have on this point.

So far, we have defined bad credit as being under 600. We also have lenders with lending requirements for credit scores of 600 and 620. Let's call the 600-639 benchmark poor credit. There is also an added array of loans, products and programs for credit scores at or above 640. Let's call the 640-659 benchmark fair credit. Many lenders require a 660 minimum credit score for conventional loans, while others are willing to go down to 620. Regardless, the 660-679 benchmarks can safely be considered average credit. Typically, conventional loan rates gradually improve at the 680, 700, 720 and 740 scores, with 740 and above being the best. So, let's call 680-719 good credit, 720-739 very good credit and 740+ excellent credit. It is quite amusing when I meet a client with a 790 credit score who gets ticked off because his/her scores are not in the 800's. While funny, you have to give those people a lot of credit for aiming high. There is nothing wrong with that.

Here is a quick summary of the credit ranges discussed:

- < 600 = Bad Credit
- 600-639 = Poor Credit
- 640-659 = Fair Credit
- 660-679 = Average Credit
- 680-719 = Good Credit
- 720-739 = Very Good Credit
- 740+ = Excellent Credit

Note: The higher the score, the lower the risk. The higher the score, the more likely you will be approved and/or qualify for a better rate.

APPENDIX C: Maintaining and improving your credit scores

- Pay bills on time.

- Get current and stay current on all payments (the last 12 months are given the most weight).

- Prepare a long term strategy.

- Keep balances low on revolving accounts. Above $0 but less than 10% of credit limit is best. Less than 30% is good. 30-50% is okay. Over 50% is not good when aiming for high scores.

- Payoff debt, don't move it around (avoid transferring all your cards onto 1 single card that will be over 50% of its credit limit).

- Don't close accounts while a balance remains.

- Don't open a lot of new accounts in a short period of time (review the marriage metaphor in Chapter 2).

- Review your credit report and check for errors annually.

- Correct errors reported on your credit report in a timely fashion.

APPENDIX D: Wait Periods after a Bankruptcy, Short Sale or Foreclosure (as of 1/2016)

CONVENTIONAL GUIDELINES

- *Foreclosure:* You may apply for a Fannie Mae (conventional) loan seven years after the sale date of your foreclosure (four years if included in bankruptcy).
- *Short Sale:* Four years with conditions.
- *Bankruptcy:* You may apply for a conventional loan after your Chapter 7 bankruptcy has been discharged for four years or two years from the discharge of a Chapter 13.

Credit must be re-established with a minimum 620 credit score, and the date of the credit report must be after the recording date of the occurrence.

FHA GUIDELINES

- *Foreclosure:* You may apply for an FHA insured loan three years after the Trust Deed (transfer) date.
- *Short Sale:* Also three years after Trust Deed date, but there is no wait period required if you can prove that you were never late on the mortgage(s) for the home that was Short Sold.
- *Bankruptcy:* You may apply for an FHA insured loan after your bankruptcy has been discharged for two years on a Chapter 7 bankruptcy.

- *Bankruptcy Chapter 13:* If you have made satisfactory bankruptcy payments for one year, then the lender may determine that you have re-established satisfactory credit. If the trustee or the bankruptcy judge approves of the issuance of new credit, the lender may give be able to give you a loan approval.

Application date must be after the date of the occurrence to be eligible for FHA financing.

VA GUIDELINES

- *Foreclosure:* You may apply for a VA loan two years after the Trust Deed (transfer) date.
- *Short Sale:* Also two years after Trust Deed date, but like FHA, there is no wait period required if you can prove that you were never late on the mortgage(s) for the home that was Short Sold.
- *Bankruptcy:* You may apply for a VA loan after your bankruptcy has been discharged for two years on a Chapter 7 bankruptcy.
- *Bankruptcy Chapter 13:* If you have made satisfactory bankruptcy payments for one year, then the lender may determine that you have re-established satisfactory credit. If the trustee or the bankruptcy judge approves of the issuance of new credit, the lender may give be able to give you a loan approval.

Credit must be re-established with a minimum 620 credit score.

Application date must be after the recording date of the occurrence to be eligible for VA financing.

USDA GUIDELINES

- *Bankruptcy:* You may apply for a USDA rural loan three years after the discharge date of a Chapter 7 bankruptcy or one year from the completion of a Chapter 13 bankruptcy.
- *Foreclosure:* You may apply for a USDA rural loan three years after the Trust Deed date.
- *Short Sale / Deed in Lieu of Foreclosure:* Same as foreclosure.

Date of credit approval must be after date of the occurrence to be eligible for USDA financing.

APPENDIX E: Mortgage Insurance (MI)

First, mortgage insurance (MI) should not be confused with homeowner's insurance (HOI). While homeowner's insurance covers you in the event that your home is burned down or robbed, mortgage insurance covers part of the lender's loss in the event that you default on your loan. So, why are you forced to buy MI when it doesn't protect you? Well, MI is what allows you to buy a home with less than 20% down. If you have 20% to put down and do not have a better use for that money, then put it down and avoid MI.

Second, MI also goes by the name MIP and PMI. MIP stands for Mortgage Insurance Premium and is the mortgage insurance associated with FHA loans. PMI stands for Private Mortgage Insurance and is associated with conventional loans. No matter what you call them, at the end of the day they are both mortgage insurances. Both are still MI!

Third, with conventional loans, there are different ways that the MI can be paid. The most common way is paid by the borrower and called Borrower Paid Mortgage Insurance (BPMI). This is the most popular option because it has the lowest upfront cost ($0) and a lower interest rate. Another common MI option is called Lender Paid Mortgage Insurance (LPMI). In this case, the lender will pay for the MI in exchange for a higher interest rate. The LPMI option is popular because the overall mortgage payment is lower than that of BPMI. While most BPMI is paid on a monthly basis, there are other options that are not recommended due to higher upfront costs/funds.

Finally, the most important thing to keep in mind regarding MI is that the monthly mortgage insurance can be taken off of a conventional loan once the loan balance drops under 80% of the purchase price (or the original appraised value if lower than purchase price). This was the case for FHA loans until June 2013. Presently, if you put less than 10% down on an FHA loan, you will have MIP for the life of the loan. This is not necessarily a bad thing, unless you plan to keep the loan for more than ten years. Before you get to that point, you may want to consider refinancing into a conventional loan sooner rather than later.

Quick side note: This appendix had a lot of acronyms. If you are getting a little lost with all these acronyms, remember there is a "cheat sheet" — Appendix F — to help out.

Acronyms/Key Terms

ARM: An Adjustable Rate Mortgage is a loan with an interest rate that is not fixed for the life of the loan. Typically, these types of loans have a rate fixed for the first few years of the loan and then adjust annually thereafter. These are popular with experienced borrowers who plan to only keep the loan for a short period of time and want to enjoy a lower rate than that on a 30-year fixed rate.

APR: Not to be confused with the loan's interest rate, which is a component of the APR, the Annual Percentage Rate calculates the cost to the applicant for the mortgage. It takes the total amount borrowed, subtracts certain fees from that amount, and calculates the interest rate without changing the payment amount. In other words, it helps to factor the total cost of your credit - the cost to get the loan (closing costs) and the cost to have the loan (interest rate).

BPMI: Borrower Paid Mortgage Insurance. See Appendix E for more details.

CFPB: The Consumer Financial Protection Bureau, an independent agency of the United States government, is responsible for consumer protection in the financial sector.

CLTV: Combined-Loan-to-Value is the total percentage of all mortgages to the value of the property.

DTI: Debt-to-Income is the ratio of the borrower's gross monthly income to their consumer and/or housing debt.

FCRA: The Fair Credit Reporting Act is the U.S. federal government legislation enacted to promote the accuracy, fairness, and privacy of consumer information contained in the files of consumer reporting-agencies.

FHA: The Federal Housing Administration is a federal government agency that oversees the U.S. housing market. FHA mortgages are guaranteed by the federal government and offered by lenders.

FHLMC/Freddie Mac: The Federal Home Loan Mortgage Corporation is one of two GSE's (Government Sponsored Enterprises) created by Congress to increase access to mortgages. Mortgages offered under Freddie Mac guidelines are also called "conforming" mortgages since they conform to Freddie Mac guidelines for conventional loans. In other words, the FHLMC make the rules for conventional loans.

FNMA/Fannie Mae: The Federal National Mortgage Association, like Freddie Mac, is a GSE that was created by Congress to increase access to mortgages. Mortgages offered under Fannie Mae guidelines are called "conforming" mortgages since they conform to Fannie Mae guidelines.

FTHB: First Time Home Buyer is a buyer who has not had an ownership interest in a residence within the previous three years.

GNMA/Ginnie Mae: The Government National Mortgage Association is the guarantee agency for the federally-guaranteed mortgages offered through the VA, FHA, and USDA.

HUD: Housing and Urban Development is the cabinet department of the federal government that helps oversee the U.S. housing market. All laws that are passed by Congress are administered by HUD.

LO: The Loan Officer is outlined in Chapter 1. Also see MLO.

LPMI: Lender Paid Mortgage Insurance is mortgage insurance paid by the lender instead of the borrower. This is accomplished by the lender increasing the mortgage's interest rate.

LTV: Loan-to-Value is the percentage of the mortgage loan balance to the home's value.

MIP: Mortgage Insurance Premium is similar to PMI but is used for FHA mortgages. With FHA mortgages, there is an upfront MIP payment as well as a monthly MI payment.

MLO: Mortgage Loan Originator. Any individual who, for compensation or gain, takes a residential mortgage loan application or offers or negotiates terms of a residential mortgage loan application must be licensed or registered as a mortgage loan originator.

PITI: Principal-Interest-Taxes-Insurance. This figure is used to determine the housing expense for the loan application. These variables can also be part of the mortgage payment.

PMI: Private Mortgage Insurance. See Appendix E.

Refi: Short for refinance. A refinance is when a new mortgage is taken out to pay off another mortgage. This is done for numerous reasons (to get a better loan, take cash out, remove or add a borrower).

VA: The Veterans Administration, like FHA, has mortgages guaranteed by the federal government and offered by lenders. VA mortgages are only available to members of the military and widows of veterans.

USDA: The United States Department of Agriculture, like FHA, has mortgages guaranteed by the federal government and offered by lenders.

VOD: Verification of Deposit is a form sent to the bank/credit union/savings bank to verify the amount of funds in the account and to provide an average balance over a specified period of time.

VOE: Verification of Employment is a form that is sent to the employer to verify employment. It is common to also have a VOE done verbally by the lender just prior to closing.

VOR: Verification of Rent is a form that is sent to the landlord to verify the timely payment of rent.

W2: W2's are the tax forms provided by an employer to report the total year's income of an individual.

1099: 1099's are the tax forms provided by an institution to report the total year's income.

4506-T: This is a Request for Tax Transcript form, which allows the lenders to retrieve transcripts of tax returns that are on file with the IRS in order to verify that the tax returns provided for qualifying for the mortgage are valid.